The Real Estate

Open House

Guest Book

Christine Dunne

Donegal Publishing Company

Los Angeles, California 2020

ISBN 978-0-9788128-8-1

Printed by Lulu Press, Inc. in the United States of America

First Printing, 2020

Donegal Publishing Company

1850 Industrial Street, #307

Los Angeles, California, 90021

www.deadland.co

Name_____ Date_____

Phone number_____ Email_____

_____

_____

_____

Name_____ Date_____

Phone number_____ Email_____

_____

_____

_____

Name_____ Date_____

Phone number_____ Email_____

_____

_____

_____

Name_____ Date_____

Phone number_____ Email_____

_____

_____

_____

Name_____ Date_____

Phone number_____ Email_____

_____

_____

_____

Name_____ Date_____

Phone number_____ Email_____

_____

_____

_____

Name_____ Date_____

Phone number_____ Email_____

_____

_____

_____

Name_____ Date_____

Phone number_____ Email_____

_____

_____

_____

Name_____ Date_____

Phone number_____ Email_____

_____

_____

_____

Name_____ Date_____

Phone number_____ Email_____

_____

_____

_____

Name_____ Date_____

Phone number_____ Email_____

_____

_____

_____

Name_____ Date_____

Phone number_____ Email_____

_____

_____

_____

Name_____ Date_____

Phone number_____ Email_____

_____

_____

_____

Name_____ Date_____

Phone number_____ Email_____

_____

_____

_____

Name_____ Date_____

Phone number_____ Email_____

_____

_____

_____

Name_____ Date_____

Phone number_____ Email_____

_____

_____

_____

Name_____ Date_____

Phone number_____ Email_____

_____

_____

_____

Name_____ Date_____

Phone number_____ Email_____

_____

_____

_____

Name_____ Date_____

Phone number_____ Email_____

_____

_____

_____

Name_____ Date_____

Phone number_____ Email_____

_____

_____

_____

Name_____ Date_____

Phone number_____ Email_____

_____

_____

_____

Name_____ Date_____

Phone number_____ Email_____

_____

_____

_____

Name_____ Date_____

Phone number_____ Email_____

_____

_____

_____

Name_____ Date_____

Phone number_____ Email_____

_____

_____

_____

Name_____ Date_____

Phone number_____ Email_____

_____

_____

_____

Name_____ Date_____

Phone number_____ Email_____

_____

_____

_____

Name_____ Date_____

Phone number_____ Email_____

_____

_____

_____

Name_____ Date_____

Phone number_____ Email_____

_____

_____

_____

Name_____ Date_____

Phone number_____ Email_____

_____

_____

_____

Name_____ Date_____

Phone number_____ Email_____

_____

_____

_____

Name_____ Date_____

Phone number_____ Email_____

_____

_____

_____

Name_____ Date_____

Phone number_____ Email_____

_____

_____

_____

Name_____ Date_____

Phone number_____ Email_____

_____

_____

_____

Name_____ Date_____

Phone number_____ Email_____

_____

_____

_____

Name_____ Date_____

Phone number_____ Email_____

_____

_____

_____

Name_____ Date_____

Phone number_____ Email_____

_____

_____

_____

Name_____ Date_____

Phone number_____ Email_____

_____

_____

_____

Name_____ Date_____

Phone number_____ Email_____

_____

_____

_____

Name_____ Date_____

Phone number_____ Email_____

_____

_____

_____

Name_____ Date_____

Phone number_____ Email_____

_____

_____

_____

Name_____ Date_____

Phone number_____ Email_____

_____

_____

_____

Name_____ Date_____

Phone number_____ Email_____

_____

_____

_____

Name_____ Date_____

Phone number_____ Email_____

_____

_____

_____

Name_____ Date_____

Phone number_____ Email_____

_____

_____

_____

Name_____ Date_____

Phone number_____ Email_____

_____

_____

_____

Name_____ Date_____

Phone number_____ Email_____

_____

_____

_____

Name_____ Date_____

Phone number_____ Email_____

_____

_____

_____

Name_____ Date_____

Phone number_____ Email_____

_____

_____

_____

Name_____ Date_____

Phone number_____ Email_____

_____

_____

_____

Name_____ Date_____

Phone number_____ Email_____

_____

_____

_____

Name_____ Date_____

Phone number_____ Email_____

_____

_____

_____

Name_____ Date_____

Phone number_____ Email_____

_____

_____

_____

Name_____ Date_____

Phone number_____ Email_____

_____

_____

_____

Name_____ Date_____

Phone number_____ Email_____

_____

_____

_____

Name_____ Date_____

Phone number_____ Email_____

_____

_____

_____

Name_____ Date_____

Phone number_____ Email_____

_____

_____

_____

Name_____ Date_____

Phone number_____ Email_____

_____

_____

_____

Name_____ Date_____

Phone number_____ Email_____

_____

_____

_____

Name_____ Date_____

Phone number_____ Email_____

_____

_____

_____

Name_____ Date_____

Phone number_____ Email_____

_____

_____

_____

Name_____ Date_____

Phone number_____ Email_____

_____

_____

_____

Name_____ Date_____

Phone number_____ Email_____

_____

_____

_____

Name_____ Date_____

Phone number_____ Email_____

_____

_____

_____

Name_____ Date_____

Phone number_____ Email_____

_____

_____

_____

Name_____ Date_____

Phone number_____ Email_____

_____

_____

_____

Name_____ Date_____

Phone number_____ Email_____

_____

_____

_____

Name_____ Date_____

Phone number_____ Email_____

_____

_____

_____

Name_____ Date_____

Phone number_____ Email_____

_____

_____

_____

Name_____ Date_____

Phone number_____ Email_____

_____

_____

_____

Name_____ Date_____

Phone number_____ Email_____

_____

_____

_____

Name_____ Date_____

Phone number_____ Email_____

_____

_____

_____

Name_____ Date_____

Phone number_____ Email_____

_____

_____

_____

Name_____ Date_____

Phone number_____ Email_____

_____

_____

_____

Name_____ Date_____

Phone number_____ Email_____

_____

_____

_____

Name_____ Date_____

Phone number_____ Email_____

_____

_____

_____

Name_____ Date_____

Phone number_____ Email_____

_____

_____

_____

Name_____ Date_____

Phone number_____ Email_____

_____

_____

_____

Name_____ Date_____

Phone number_____ Email_____

_____

_____

_____

Name_____ Date_____

Phone number_____ Email_____

_____

_____

_____

Name_____ Date_____

Phone number_____ Email_____

_____

_____

_____

Name_____ Date_____

Phone number_____ Email_____

_____

_____

_____

Name_____ Date_____

Phone number_____ Email_____

_____

_____

_____

Name_____ Date_____

Phone number_____ Email_____

_____

_____

_____

Name_____ Date_____

Phone number_____ Email_____

_____

_____

_____

Name_____ Date_____

Phone number_____ Email_____

_____

_____

_____

Name_____ Date_____

Phone number_____ Email_____

_____

_____

_____

Name_____ Date_____

Phone number_____ Email_____

_____

_____

_____

Name_____ Date_____

Phone number_____ Email_____

_____

_____

_____

Name_____ Date_____

Phone number_____ Email_____

_____

_____

_____

Name_____ Date_____

Phone number_____ Email_____

_____

_____

_____

Name_____ Date_____

Phone number_____ Email_____

_____

_____

_____

Name_____ Date_____

Phone number_____ Email_____

_____

_____

_____

Name_____ Date_____

Phone number_____ Email_____

_____

_____

_____

Name_____ Date_____

Phone number_____ Email_____

_____

_____

_____

Name_____ Date_____

Phone number_____ Email_____

_____

_____

_____

Name_____ Date_____

Phone number_____ Email_____

_____

_____

_____

Name_____ Date_____

Phone number_____ Email_____

_____

_____

_____

Name_____ Date_____

Phone number_____ Email_____

_____

_____

_____

Name_____ Date_____

Phone number_____ Email_____

_____

_____

Name_____ Date_____

Phone number_____ Email_____

_____

_____

_____

Name_____ Date_____

Phone number_____ Email_____

_____

_____

_____

Name_____ Date_____

Phone number_____ Email_____

_____

_____

_____

Name_____ Date_____

Phone number_____ Email_____

_____

_____

_____

Name_____ Date_____

Phone number_____ Email_____

_____

_____

_____

Name_____ Date_____

Phone number_____ Email_____

_____

_____

_____

Name_____ Date_____

Phone number_____ Email_____

_____

_____

_____

Name_____ Date_____

Phone number_____ Email_____

_____

_____

_____

Name_____ Date_____

Phone number_____ Email_____

_____

_____

_____

Name_____ Date_____

Phone number_____ Email_____

_____

_____

_____

Name_____ Date_____

Phone number_____ Email_____

_____

_____

_____

Name_____ Date_____

Phone number_____ Email_____

_____

_____

_____

Name_____ Date_____

Phone number_____ Email_____

_____

_____

_____

Name_____ Date_____

Phone number_____ Email_____

_____

_____

_____

Name_____ Date_____

Phone number_____ Email_____

_____

_____

_____

Name_____ Date_____

Phone number_____ Email_____

_____

_____

_____

Name_____ Date_____

Phone number_____ Email_____

_____

_____

_____

Name_____ Date_____

Phone number_____ Email_____

_____

_____

_____

Name_____ Date_____

Phone number_____ Email_____

_____

_____

_____

Name_____ Date_____

Phone number_____ Email_____

_____

_____

_____

Name_____ Date_____

Phone number_____ Email_____

_____

_____

_____

Name_____ Date_____

Phone number_____ Email_____

_____

_____

_____

Name_____ Date_____

Phone number_____ Email_____

_____

_____

_____

Name_____ Date_____

Phone number_____ Email_____

_____

_____

_____

Name_____ Date_____

Phone number_____ Email_____

_____

_____

_____

Name_____ Date_____

Phone number_____ Email_____

_____

_____

_____

Name_____ Date_____

Phone number_____ Email_____

_____

_____

_____

Name_____ Date_____

Phone number_____ Email_____

_____

_____

_____

Name_____ Date_____

Phone number_____ Email_____

_____

_____

_____

Name_____ Date_____

Phone number_____ Email_____

_____

_____

_____

Name_____ Date_____

Phone number_____ Email_____

_____

_____

_____

Name_____ Date_____

Phone number_____ Email_____

_____

_____

_____

Name_____ Date_____

Phone number_____ Email_____

_____

_____

_____

Name_____ Date_____

Phone number_____ Email_____

_____

_____

_____

Name_____ Date_____

Phone number_____ Email_____

_____

_____

_____

Name_____ Date_____

Phone number_____ Email_____

_____

_____

_____

Name_____ Date_____

Phone number_____ Email_____

_____

_____

_____

Name_____ Date_____

Phone number_____ Email_____

_____

_____

_____

Name_____ Date_____

Phone number_____ Email_____

_____

_____

_____

Name_____ Date_____

Phone number_____ Email_____

_____

_____

_____

Name_____ Date_____

Phone number_____ Email_____

_____

_____

_____

Name_____ Date_____

Phone number_____ Email_____

_____

_____

_____

Name_____ Date_____

Phone number_____ Email_____

_____

_____

_____

Name_____ Date_____

Phone number_____ Email_____

_____

_____

_____

Name_____ Date_____

Phone number_____ Email_____

_____

_____

_____

Name_____ Date_____

Phone number_____ Email_____

_____

_____

_____

Name_____ Date_____

Phone number_____ Email_____

_____

_____

_____

Name_____ Date_____

Phone number_____ Email_____

_____

_____

_____

Name_____ Date_____

Phone number_____ Email_____

_____

_____

_____

Name_____ Date_____

Phone number_____ Email_____

_____

_____

_____

Name_____ Date_____

Phone number_____ Email_____

_____

_____

_____

Name_____ Date_____

Phone number_____ Email_____

_____

_____

_____

Name_____ Date_____

Phone number_____ Email_____

_____

_____

_____

Name_____ Date_____

Phone number_____ Email_____

_____

_____

_____

Name_____ Date_____

Phone number_____ Email_____

_____

_____

_____

Name_____ Date_____

Phone number_____ Email_____

_____

_____

_____

Name_____ Date_____

Phone number_____ Email_____

_____

_____

_____

Name_____ Date_____

Phone number_____ Email_____

_____

_____

_____

Name_____ Date_____

Phone number_____ Email_____

_____

_____

_____

Name_____ Date_____

Phone number_____ Email_____

_____

_____

_____

Name_____ Date_____

Phone number_____ Email_____

_____

_____

_____

Name_____ Date_____

Phone number_____ Email_____

_____

_____

_____

Name_____ Date_____

Phone number_____ Email_____

_____

_____

_____

Name_____ Date_____

Phone number_____ Email_____

_____

_____

_____

Name_____ Date_____

Phone number_____ Email_____

_____

_____

_____

Name_____ Date_____

Phone number_____ Email_____

_____

_____

_____

Name_____ Date_____

Phone number_____ Email_____

_____

_____

_____

Name_____ Date_____

Phone number_____ Email_____

_____

_____

_____

Name_____ Date_____

Phone number_____ Email_____

_____

_____

_____

Name_____ Date_____

Phone number_____ Email_____

_____

_____

_____

Name_____ Date_____

Phone number_____ Email_____

_____

_____

_____

Name_____ Date_____

Phone number_____ Email_____

_____

_____

_____

Name_____ Date_____

Phone number_____ Email_____

_____

_____

_____

Name_____ Date_____

Phone number_____ Email_____

_____

_____

_____

Name_____ Date_____

Phone number_____ Email_____

_____

_____

_____

Name_____ Date_____

Phone number_____ Email_____

_____

_____

_____

Name_____ Date_____

Phone number_____ Email_____

_____

_____

_____

Name_____ Date_____

Phone number_____ Email_____

_____

_____

_____

Name_____ Date_____

Phone number_____ Email_____

_____

_____

_____

Name_____ Date_____

Phone number_____ Email_____

_____

_____

_____

Name_____ Date_____

Phone number_____ Email_____

_____

_____

_____

Name_____ Date_____

Phone number_____ Email_____

_____

_____

_____

Name_____ Date_____

Phone number_____ Email_____

_____

_____

_____

Name_____ Date_____

Phone number_____ Email_____

_____

_____

_____

Name_____ Date_____

Phone number_____ Email_____

_____

_____

_____

Name_____ Date_____

Phone number_____ Email_____

_____

_____

_____

Name_____ Date_____

Phone number_____ Email_____

_____

_____

_____

Name_____ Date_____

Phone number_____ Email_____

_____

_____

_____

Name_____ Date_____

Phone number_____ Email_____

_____

_____

_____

Name_____ Date_____

Phone number_____ Email_____

_____

_____

_____

Name_____ Date_____

Phone number_____ Email_____

_____

_____

_____

Name_____ Date_____

Phone number_____ Email_____

_____

_____

_____

Name_____ Date_____

Phone number_____ Email_____

_____

_____

_____

Name_____ Date_____

Phone number_____ Email_____

_____

_____

_____

Name_____ Date_____

Phone number_____ Email_____

_____

_____

_____

Name_____ Date_____

Phone number_____ Email_____

_____

_____

_____

Name_____ Date_____

Phone number_____ Email_____

_____

_____

_____

Name_____ Date_____

Phone number_____ Email_____

_____

_____

_____

Name_____ Date_____

Phone number_____ Email_____

_____

_____

_____

Name_____ Date_____

Phone number_____ Email_____

_____

_____

_____

Name_____ Date_____

Phone number_____ Email_____

_____

_____

_____

Name_____ Date_____

Phone number_____ Email_____

_____

_____

_____

Name_____ Date_____

Phone number_____ Email_____

_____

_____

_____

Name_____ Date_____

Phone number_____ Email_____

_____

_____

_____

Name_____ Date_____

Phone number_____ Email_____

_____

_____

_____

Name_____ Date_____

Phone number_____ Email_____

_____

_____

_____

Name_____ Date_____

Phone number_____ Email_____

_____

_____

_____

Name_____ Date_____

Phone number_____ Email_____

_____

_____

_____

Name_____ Date_____

Phone number_____ Email_____

_____

_____

_____

Name_____ Date_____

Phone number_____ Email_____

_____

_____

_____

Name_____ Date_____

Phone number_____ Email_____

_____

_____

_____

Name_____ Date_____

Phone number_____ Email_____

_____

_____

_____

Name_____ Date_____

Phone number_____ Email_____

_____

_____

_____

Name_____ Date_____

Phone number_____ Email_____

_____

_____

_____

Name_____ Date_____

Phone number_____ Email_____

_____

_____

_____

Name_____ Date_____

Phone number_____ Email_____

_____

_____

_____

Name_____ Date_____

Phone number_____ Email_____

_____

_____

_____

Name_____ Date_____

Phone number_____ Email_____

_____

_____

_____

Name_____ Date_____

Phone number_____ Email_____

_____

_____

_____

Name_____ Date_____

Phone number_____ Email_____

_____

_____

_____

Name_____ Date_____

Phone number_____ Email_____

_____

_____

_____

Name_____ Date_____

Phone number_____ Email_____

_____

_____

_____

Name_____ Date_____

Phone number_____ Email_____

_____

_____

_____

Name_____ Date_____

Phone number_____ Email_____

_____

_____

_____

Name_____ Date_____

Phone number_____ Email_____

_____

_____

_____

Name_____ Date_____

Phone number_____ Email_____

_____

_____

_____

Name_____ Date_____

Phone number_____ Email_____

_____

_____

_____

Name_____ Date_____

Phone number_____ Email_____

_____

_____

_____

Name_____ Date_____

Phone number_____ Email_____

_____

_____

_____

Name_____ Date_____

Phone number_____ Email_____

_____

_____

_____

Name_____ Date_____

Phone number_____ Email_____

_____

_____

_____

Name_____ Date_____

Phone number_____ Email_____

_____

_____

_____

Name_____ Date_____

Phone number_____ Email_____

_____

_____

_____

Name_____ Date_____

Phone number_____ Email_____

_____

_____

_____

Name_____ Date_____

Phone number_____ Email_____

_____

_____

_____

Name_____ Date_____

Phone number_____ Email_____

_____

_____

_____

Name_____ Date_____

Phone number_____ Email_____

_____

_____

_____

Name_____ Date_____

Phone number_____ Email_____

_____

_____

_____

Name_____ Date_____

Phone number_____ Email_____

_____

_____

_____

Name_____ Date_____

Phone number_____ Email_____

_____

_____

_____

Name_____ Date_____

Phone number_____ Email_____

_____

_____

_____

Name_____ Date_____

Phone number_____ Email_____

_____

_____

_____

Name_____ Date_____

Phone number_____ Email_____

_____

_____

_____

Name_____ Date_____

Phone number_____ Email_____

_____

_____

_____

Name_____ Date_____

Phone number_____ Email_____

_____

_____

_____

Name_____ Date_____

Phone number_____ Email_____

_____

_____

_____

Name_____ Date_____

Phone number_____ Email_____

_____

_____

_____

Name_____ Date_____

Phone number_____ Email_____

_____

_____

_____

Name_____ Date_____

Phone number_____ Email_____

_____

_____

_____

Name_____ Date_____

Phone number_____ Email_____

_____

_____

_____

Name_____ Date_____

Phone number_____ Email_____

_____

_____

_____

Name_____ Date_____

Phone number_____ Email_____

_____

_____

_____

Name_____ Date_____

Phone number_____ Email_____

_____

_____

_____

Name_____ Date_____

Phone number_____ Email_____

_____

_____

_____

Name_____ Date_____

Phone number_____ Email_____

_____

_____

_____

Name_____ Date_____

Phone number_____ Email_____

_____

_____

_____

Name_____ Date_____

Phone number_____ Email_____

_____

_____

_____

Name_____ Date_____

Phone number_____ Email_____

_____

_____

_____

Name_____ Date_____

Phone number_____ Email_____

_____

_____

_____

Name_____ Date_____

Phone number_____ Email_____

_____

_____

_____

Name_____ Date_____

Phone number_____ Email_____

_____

_____

_____

Name_____ Date_____

Phone number_____ Email_____

_____

_____

_____

Name_____ Date_____

Phone number_____ Email_____

_____

_____

_____

Name_____ Date_____

Phone number_____ Email_____

_____

_____

_____

Name_____ Date_____

Phone number_____ Email_____

_____

_____

_____

Name_____ Date_____

Phone number_____ Email_____

_____

_____

_____

Name_____ Date_____

Phone number_____ Email_____

_____

_____

_____

Name_____ Date_____

Phone number_____ Email_____

_____

_____

_____

Name_____ Date_____

Phone number_____ Email_____

_____

_____

_____

Name_____ Date_____

Phone number_____ Email_____

_____

_____

_____

Name_____ Date_____

Phone number_____ Email_____

_____

_____

_____

Name_____ Date_____

Phone number_____ Email_____

_____

_____

_____

Name_____ Date_____

Phone number_____ Email_____

_____

_____

_____

Name_____ Date_____

Phone number_____ Email_____

_____

_____

_____

Name_____ Date_____

Phone number_____ Email_____

_____

_____

_____

Name_____ Date_____

Phone number_____ Email_____

_____

_____

_____

Name_____ Date_____

Phone number_____ Email_____

_____

_____

_____

Name_____ Date_____

Phone number_____ Email_____

_____

_____

_____

Name_____ Date_____

Phone number_____ Email_____

_____

_____

_____

Name_____ Date_____

Phone number_____ Email_____

_____

_____

_____

Name_____ Date_____

Phone number_____ Email_____

_____

_____

_____

Name_____ Date_____

Phone number_____ Email_____

_____

_____

_____

Name_____ Date_____

Phone number_____ Email_____

_____

_____

_____

Name_____ Date_____

Phone number_____ Email_____

_____

_____

_____

Name_____ Date_____

Phone number_____ Email_____

_____

_____

_____

Name_____ Date_____

Phone number_____ Email_____

_____

_____

_____

Name_____ Date_____

Phone number_____ Email_____

_____

_____

_____

Name_____ Date_____

Phone number_____ Email_____

_____

_____

_____

Name_____ Date_____

Phone number_____ Email_____

_____

_____

_____

Name_____ Date_____

Phone number_____ Email_____

_____

_____

_____

Name_____ Date_____

Phone number_____ Email_____

_____

_____

_____

Name_____ Date_____

Phone number_____ Email_____

_____

_____

_____

Name_____ Date_____

Phone number_____ Email_____

_____

_____

_____

Name_____ Date_____

Phone number_____ Email_____

_____

_____

_____

Name_____ Date_____

Phone number_____ Email_____

_____

_____

_____

Name_____ Date_____

Phone number_____ Email_____

_____

_____

_____

Name_____ Date_____

Phone number_____ Email_____

_____

_____

_____

Name_____ Date_____

Phone number_____ Email_____

_____

_____

_____

Name_____ Date_____

Phone number_____ Email_____

_____

_____

_____

Name_____ Date_____

Phone number_____ Email_____

_____

_____

_____

Name_____ Date_____

Phone number_____ Email_____

_____

_____

_____

Name_____ Date_____

Phone number_____ Email_____

_____

_____

_____

Name_____ Date_____

Phone number_____ Email_____

_____

_____

_____

Name_____ Date_____

Phone number_____ Email_____

_____

_____

_____

Name_____ Date_____

Phone number_____ Email_____

_____

_____

_____

Name_____ Date_____

Phone number_____ Email_____

_____

_____

_____

Name_____ Date_____

Phone number_____ Email_____

_____

_____

_____

Name_____ Date_____

Phone number_____ Email_____

_____

_____

_____

Name_____ Date_____

Phone number_____ Email_____

_____

_____

_____

Name_____ Date_____

Phone number_____ Email_____

_____

_____

_____

Name_____ Date_____

Phone number_____ Email_____

_____

_____

_____

Name_____ Date_____

Phone number_____ Email_____

_____

_____

_____

Name_____ Date_____

Phone number_____ Email_____

_____

_____

_____

Name_____ Date_____

Phone number_____ Email_____

_____

_____

_____

Name_____ Date_____

Phone number_____ Email_____

_____

_____

_____

Name_____ Date_____

Phone number_____ Email_____

_____

_____

_____

Name_____ Date_____

Phone number_____ Email_____

_____

_____

_____

Name_____ Date_____

Phone number_____ Email_____

_____

_____

_____

Name_____ Date_____

Phone number_____ Email_____

_____

_____

_____

Name_____ Date_____

Phone number_____ Email_____

_____

_____

_____

Name_____ Date_____

Phone number_____ Email_____

_____

_____

_____

Name_____ Date_____

Phone number_____ Email_____

_____

_____

_____

Name_____ Date_____

Phone number_____ Email_____

_____

_____

_____

Name_____ Date_____

Phone number_____ Email_____

_____

_____

_____

Name_____ Date_____

Phone number_____ Email_____

_____

_____

_____

Name_____ Date_____

Phone number_____ Email_____

_____

_____

_____

Name_____ Date_____

Phone number_____ Email_____

_____

_____

_____

Name_____ Date_____

Phone number_____ Email_____

_____

_____

_____

Name_____ Date_____

Phone number_____ Email_____

_____

_____

_____

Name_____ Date_____

Phone number_____ Email_____

_____

_____

_____

Name_____ Date_____

Phone number_____ Email_____

_____

_____

_____

Name_____ Date_____

Phone number_____ Email_____

_____

_____

_____

Name_____ Date_____

Phone number_____ Email_____

_____

_____

_____

Name_____ Date_____

Phone number_____ Email_____

_____

_____

_____

Name_____ Date_____

Phone number_____ Email_____

_____

_____

_____

Name_____ Date_____

Phone number_____ Email_____

_____

_____

_____

Name_____ Date_____

Phone number_____ Email_____

_____

_____

_____

Name_____ Date_____

Phone number_____ Email_____

_____

_____

_____

Name_____ Date_____

Phone number_____ Email_____

_____

_____

_____

Name_____ Date_____

Phone number_____ Email_____

_____

_____

_____

Name_____ Date_____

Phone number_____ Email_____

_____

_____

_____

Name_____ Date_____

Phone number_____ Email_____

_____

_____

_____

Name_____ Date_____

Phone number_____ Email_____

_____

_____

_____

Name_____ Date_____

Phone number_____ Email_____

_____

_____

_____

Name_____ Date_____

Phone number_____ Email_____

_____

_____

_____

Name_____ Date_____

Phone number_____ Email_____

_____

_____

_____

Name_____ Date_____

Phone number_____ Email_____

_____

_____

_____

Name_____ Date_____

Phone number_____ Email_____

_____

_____

_____

Name_____ Date_____

Phone number_____ Email_____

_____

_____

_____

Name_____ Date_____

Phone number_____ Email_____

_____

_____

_____

Name_____ Date_____

Phone number_____ Email_____

_____

_____

_____

Name_____ Date_____

Phone number_____ Email_____

_____

_____

_____

Name_____ Date_____

Phone number_____ Email_____

_____

_____

_____

Name_____ Date_____

Phone number_____ Email_____

_____

_____

_____

Name_____ Date_____

Phone number_____ Email_____

_____

_____

_____

Name_____ Date_____

Phone number_____ Email_____

_____

_____

_____

Name_____ Date_____

Phone number_____ Email_____

_____

_____

_____

Name_____ Date_____

Phone number_____ Email_____

_____

_____

_____

Name_____ Date_____

Phone number_____ Email_____

_____

_____

_____

Name_____ Date_____

Phone number_____ Email_____

_____

_____

_____

Name_____ Date_____

Phone number_____ Email_____

_____

_____

_____

Name_____ Date_____

Phone number_____ Email_____

_____

_____

_____

Name_____ Date_____

Phone number_____ Email_____

_____

_____

_____

Name_____ Date_____

Phone number_____ Email_____

_____

_____

_____

Name_____ Date_____

Phone number_____ Email_____

_____

_____

_____

Name_____ Date_____

Phone number_____ Email_____

_____

_____

_____

Name_____ Date_____

Phone number_____ Email_____

_____

_____

_____

Name_____ Date_____

Phone number_____ Email_____

_____

_____

_____

Name_____ Date_____

Phone number_____ Email_____

_____

_____

_____

Name_____ Date_____

Phone number_____ Email_____

_____

_____

_____

Name_____ Date_____

Phone number_____ Email_____

_____

_____

_____

Name_____ Date_____

Phone number_____ Email_____

_____

_____

_____

Name_____ Date_____

Phone number_____ Email_____

_____

_____

_____

Name_____ Date_____

Phone number_____ Email_____

_____

_____

_____

Name_____ Date_____

Phone number_____ Email_____

_____

_____

_____

Name_____ Date_____

Phone number_____ Email_____

_____

_____

_____

Name_____ Date_____

Phone number_____ Email_____

_____

_____

_____

Name_____ Date_____

Phone number_____ Email_____

_____

_____

_____

Name_____ Date_____

Phone number_____ Email_____

_____

_____

_____

Name_____ Date_____

Phone number_____ Email_____

_____

_____

_____

Name_____ Date_____

Phone number_____ Email_____

_____

_____

_____

Name_____ Date_____

Phone number_____ Email_____

_____

_____

_____

Name_____ Date_____

Phone number_____ Email_____

_____

_____

_____

Name_____ Date_____

Phone number_____ Email_____

_____

_____

_____

Name_____ Date_____

Phone number_____ Email_____

_____

_____

_____

Name_____ Date_____

Phone number_____ Email_____

_____

_____

_____

Name_____ Date_____

Phone number_____ Email_____

_____

_____

_____

Name_____ Date_____

Phone number_____ Email_____

_____

_____

_____

Name_____ Date_____

Phone number_____ Email_____

_____

_____

_____

Name_____ Date_____

Phone number_____ Email_____

_____

_____

_____

Name_____ Date_____

Phone number_____ Email_____

_____

_____

_____

Name_____ Date_____

Phone number_____ Email_____

_____

_____

_____

Name_____ Date_____

Phone number_____ Email_____

_____

_____

_____

Name_____ Date_____

Phone number_____ Email_____

_____

_____

_____

Name_____ Date_____

Phone number_____ Email_____

_____

_____

_____

Name_____ Date_____

Phone number_____ Email_____

_____

_____

_____

Name_____ Date_____

Phone number_____ Email_____

_____

_____

_____

Name_____ Date_____

Phone number_____ Email_____

_____

_____

_____

Name_____ Date_____

Phone number_____ Email_____

_____

_____

_____

Name_____ Date_____

Phone number_____ Email_____

_____

_____

_____

Name_____ Date_____

Phone number_____ Email_____

_____

_____

_____

Name_____ Date_____

Phone number_____ Email_____

_____

_____

_____

Name_____ Date_____

Phone number_____ Email_____

_____

_____

_____

Name_____ Date_____

Phone number_____ Email_____

_____

_____

_____

Name_____ Date_____

Phone number_____ Email_____

_____

_____

_____

Name_____ Date_____

Phone number_____ Email_____

_____

_____

_____

Name_____ Date_____

Phone number_____ Email_____

_____

_____

_____

Name_____ Date_____

Phone number_____ Email_____

_____

_____

_____

Name_____ Date_____

Phone number_____ Email_____

_____

_____

_____

Name_____ Date_____

Phone number_____ Email_____

_____

_____

_____

Name_____ Date_____

Phone number_____ Email_____

_____

_____

_____

Name_____ Date_____

Phone number_____ Email_____

_____

_____

_____

Name_____ Date_____

Phone number_____ Email_____

_____

_____

_____

Name_____ Date_____

Phone number_____ Email_____

_____

_____

_____

Name_____ Date_____

Phone number_____ Email_____

_____

_____

_____

Name_____ Date_____

Phone number_____ Email_____

_____

_____

_____

Name_____ Date_____

Phone number_____ Email_____

_____

_____

_____

Name_____ Date_____

Phone number_____ Email_____

_____

_____

_____

Name_____ Date_____

Phone number_____ Email_____

_____

_____

_____

Name_____ Date_____

Phone number_____ Email_____

_____

_____

_____

Name_____ Date_____

Phone number_____ Email_____

_____

_____

_____

Name_____ Date_____

Phone number_____ Email_____

_____

_____

_____

Name_____ Date_____

Phone number_____ Email_____

_____

_____

_____

Name_____ Date_____

Phone number_____ Email_____

_____

_____

_____

Name_____ Date_____

Phone number_____ Email_____

_____

_____

_____

Name_____ Date_____

Phone number_____ Email_____

_____

_____

_____

Name_____ Date_____

Phone number_____ Email_____

_____

_____

_____

Name_____ Date_____

Phone number_____ Email_____

_____

_____

_____

Name_____ Date_____

Phone number_____ Email_____

_____

_____

_____

Name_____ Date_____

Phone number_____ Email_____

_____

_____

_____

Name_____ Date_____

Phone number_____ Email_____

_____

_____

_____

Name_____ Date_____

Phone number_____ Email_____

_____

_____

_____

Name_____ Date_____

Phone number_____ Email_____

_____

_____

_____

Name_____ Date_____

Phone number_____ Email_____

_____

_____

_____

Name_____ Date_____

Phone number_____ Email_____

_____

_____

_____

Name_____ Date_____

Phone number_____ Email_____

_____

_____

_____

Name_____ Date_____

Phone number_____ Email_____

_____

_____

_____

Name_____ Date_____

Phone number_____ Email_____

_____

_____

_____

Name_____ Date_____

Phone number_____ Email_____

_____

_____

_____

Name_____ Date_____

Phone number_____ Email_____

_____

_____

_____

Name_____ Date_____

Phone number_____ Email_____

_____

_____

_____

Name_____ Date_____

Phone number_____ Email_____

_____

_____

_____

Name_____ Date_____

Phone number_____ Email_____

_____

_____

_____

Name_____ Date_____

Phone number_____ Email_____

_____

_____

_____

Name_____ Date_____

Phone number_____ Email_____

_____

_____

_____

Name_____ Date_____

Phone number_____ Email_____

_____

_____

_____

Name_____ Date_____

Phone number_____ Email_____

_____

_____

_____

Name_____ Date_____

Phone number_____ Email_____

_____

_____

_____

Name_____ Date_____

Phone number_____ Email_____

_____

_____

_____

Name_____ Date_____

Phone number_____ Email_____

_____

_____

_____

Name_____ Date_____

Phone number_____ Email_____

_____

_____

_____

Name_____ Date_____

Phone number_____ Email_____

_____

_____

_____

Name_____ Date_____

Phone number_____ Email_____

_____

_____

_____

Name_____ Date_____

Phone number_____ Email_____

_____

_____

_____

Name_____ Date_____

Phone number_____ Email_____

_____

_____

_____

Name_____ Date_____

Phone number_____ Email_____

_____

_____

_____

Name_____ Date_____

Phone number_____ Email_____

_____

_____

_____

www.ingramcontent.com/pod-product-compliance
Lightning Source LLC
Chambersburg PA
CBHW080556220326
41599CB00032B/6501